BASKETBALL FOR GIRLS

The Barnes Sports Library

This library of practical sports books covers fundamentals, techniques, coaching and playing hints and equipment for each sport. Leading coaches and players have been selected to write these books, so each volume is authoritative and based upon actual experience. Photographs and drawings, or both, illustrate techniques, equipment and play.

ARCHERY
  by Reichart & Keasey
BAIT CASTING
  by Gilmer Robinson
BASEBALL
  by Daniel E. Jessee
BASKETBALL
  by Charles C. Murphy
BASKETBALL FOR GIRLS
  by Meissner & Meyers
BASKETBALL OFFICIATING
  by Dave Tobey
BETTER BADMINTON
  by Jackson & Swan
BICYCLING
  by Ruth & Raymond Benedict
BOWLING FOR ALL
  by Falcaro & Goodman
BOXING
  by Edwin L. Haislet
CHEERLEADING
  by Loken & Dypwick
FENCING
  by Joseph Vince
FIELD HOCKEY FOR GIRLS
  by Josephine T. Lees
FLY CASTING
  by Gilmer Robinson
FOOTBALL
  by W. Glenn Killinger
FUNDAMENTAL HANDBALL
  by Bernath E. Phillips
GOLF
  by Patty Berg
HOW TO TIE FLIES
  by E. C. Gregg
ICE HOCKEY
  by Edward Jeremiah
JIU-JITSU
  by Frederick P. Lowell
LACROSSE
  by Tad Stanwick
LAWN GAMES
  by John R. Tunis

PADDLE TENNIS
  by Fessenden S. Blanchard
PHYSICAL CONDITIONING
  by Stafford & Duncan
RIDING
  by J. J. Boniface
RIFLE MARKSMANSHIP
  by Lt. Wm. L. Stephens
ROLLER SKATING
  by Bob Martin
ROPING
  by Bernard S. Mason
SIX-MAN FOOTBALL
  by Ray O. Duncan
SKATING
  by Putnam & Parkinson
SKIING
  by Walter Prager
SOCCER AND SPEEDBALL
FOR GIRLS
  by Florence L. Hupprich
SOCCER
  by Samuel Fralick
SOFTBALL
  by Arthur T. Noren
SOFTBALL FOR GIRLS
  by Viola Mitchell
SWIMMING
  by R. J. H. Kiphuth
TABLE TENNIS
  by Jay Purves
TENNIS
  by Helen Jacobs
TENNIS MADE EASY
  by Lloyd Budge
TOUCH FOOTBALL
  by John V. Grombach
TRACK AND FIELD
  by Ray M. Conger
VOLLEY BALL
  by Robert Laveaga
WRESTLING
  by E. C. Gallagher

Clair Bee's Basketball Library

THE SCIENCE OF COACHING :: MAN-TO-MAN DEFENSE AND ATTACK
ZONE DEFENSE AND ATTACK :: DRILLS AND FUNDAMENTALS

Basketball

FOR GIRLS

By

WILHELMINE E. MEISSNER, M.A.

Chairman, Department of Physical Education,
Bayside High School, L. I.

and

ELIZABETH YEEND MEYERS, M.A.

Instructor of Physical Education,
New York University

A. S. BARNES & COMPANY

NEW YORK

PREFACE

AN EFFICIENT BASKETBALL TEAM is one which uses fast and well timed passes, clever dodges, quick accurate shots, well executed pivots, and purposeful floor plays.

No attempt has been made to fully cover all phases of women's basketball. The material as set up in this book is primarily for those persons who have a general basic understanding of the game. It is natural for a person to enjoy doing those things which he or she does well. It is our hope that the material contained in this book will be useful in promoting more efficient basketball players and teams.

We recommend first that an efficient health and medical examination be given each season previous to participation in the game; second, that coaching be done by trained women leaders; third, that, when possible, the referee and umpires at games be women officials rated by the Women's National Official's Rating Committee; and fourth, that the Standards in Athletics for Women, and rules as set up by the Women's Athletic Section of the American Association of Health, Physical Education and Recreation be followed.

ACKNOWLEDGMENT

THE AUTHORS wish to express their appreciation to the Misses Edythe Schluter, Helen Forstner, and Helen Wolfe, students of the Department of Women's Physical Education, School of Education, New York University, for their assistance in posing for the drawings used in this book, and to Miss Russel Huback for her help in drawing the diagrams, and to Miss Charlotte Cohen for her help in typing the manuscript.

CONTENTS

CONTENTS

CHAPTER I

HISTORY, EQUIPMENT AND TEACHING
OF BASKETBALL

A. HISTORY OF THE GAME

IT IS ESTIMATED that over ten million persons are playing basketball today in the United States and elsewhere, and large numbers of these players are young women. It was back in 1892 that Mrs. Senda Berenson Abbott, first editor of the Women's Basketball Guide, made for girls at Smith College adaptations of the game which prevail in women's basketball today. A national sub-committee on the game was appointed in 1899 by the Executive Committee of the American Association for Health, Physical Education and Recreation.

The second rules committee meeting was held in 1905, the third in 1908, and since then yearly with the exception of 1915. It meets to discuss and revise rules, and to determine policies for basketball for women throughout the country.

The original modifications of the men's game called for division of the playing court into three sections—restricting movement of players to one section of the court; this was done to guard against "physical exertion of individual players," to eliminate "star" players, and to encourage combination plays and equalization of team work. Snatching and batting the ball was not allowed. This was done to discourage rough play. No player was permitted to hold the ball for more than three seconds, this in an effort to keep the game fast. A player was permitted a three-bounce dribble.

The evolution of the guarding rules has caused the greatest change in the game as it is played today. Until 1923 guarding in the vertical plane only was permitted. In 1923 the rules were changed so that guarding was allowed in any plane so long as there was no personal contact.

While the court is still divided into sections the two-division became the official game in 1938. The center throw method of starting the ball in play was first described in the rules in 1932-33 as an

1

optional method, and remained optional until made official as the only method of starting play in 1936-37.

Basketball is a vigorous game requiring speed and stamina. In a study made recently it was found that college women run anywhere from two to two and one-half miles in a single game which lasts thirty-two minutes. Assuredly the person whose sole activity is a walk to and from the train morning and night cannot play this game and enjoy it.

Consequently, basketball is played very largely by girls in schools and colleges and by business and professional women who enjoy vigorous activity and have the opportunity to play. Girls' clubs and church clubs in many instances offer basketball and many industrial concerns make provision for it among their youthful employees. Many girls play for a year or two after leaving school, but those who continue it for more years are in the minority.

Since basketball is primarily a game played by people of about school age the basketball committee has concerned itself with making the game more enjoyable for this group. Women's athletics is never as interesting to watch as men's athletics. Women have neither the speed, nor the strength which makes a man's contest exciting from the spectator's seat. Consequently "audience appeal" or "audience reaction" does not influence the committee in formulating rules. The concern is for the players.

You may ask, "How does the committee know what players throughout the country want and need? The National Rules Committee is composed of a group of fifteen women. Each state has a chairman and each state is organized into committees which report to the National Chairman. Each year the State Chairman submits a report of conditions in her state with recommendations for rules changes which she has culled from meetings with coaches in her state. Every recommendation is considered at the Annual Rules Revision Meeting.

In 1932 a survey was conducted by the Basketball Committee. It was found that for every man coaching women's basketball, there were six women, while 92.76 per cent of the teams playing were using the Women's Rules and 66 per cent employed women officials. In 1936 the survey was repeated and it was found that 96.40 per cent of all women playing were using the official Women's Rules. In 1937 after summarizing state reports it was found that in all but two states the use of the women's Official Rules was on the increase.

Basketball is played by women in other countries, as well as the United States and Canada. The rules have been translated into Italian, Spanish, and the Japanese, and from correspondence with people in Argentina we learn that South America is fast becoming a continent of basketball players.

B. COURTS AND EQUIPMENT

It is needless to go into detail concerning the official requirements and dimensions of basketball courts, backboards and balls, since these are given in the Official Basketball Rules for Women. It is interesting, however, to see how equipment has changed as the game has developed.

Baskets.

Baskets were originally closed at the bottom. How much playing time must have been consumed while the players waited for a referee to climb a ladder to get the ball out of the basket after each goal was scored! While open bottom baskets were introduced in 1908 the "Official Basketball Goals," closed at the bottom, were still being advertised in the Official Guides in 1918. Possibly the reason their use persisted for so long was due to the entertainment afforded by the referee as he climbed up, plucked the ball out of the basket and climbed down again.

Ball.

When Dr. Naismith, who formulated the rules for basketball for men in 1892, threw the ball into the center of the field—for this was the original method of starting play—the 18 to 100 players (there were 9 to 60 on a team) rushed to gain possession of a *football*. Today one examines balls critically to see if they are truly round, if they bounce "true" or if there is a dead spot as they hit the floor. Today we see beautiful brown or white leather balls bouncing perfectly. Certainly we cannot attribute our poor passes or shots to poorly constructed balls.

Backboards.

Backboards were originally made of wire mesh. Today they are constructed of wood or plate glass.

In addition to these necessary pieces of equipment one finds elaborate score boards, scorer's tables, timer's devices, etc. While these accessories are interesting and may add to the enjoyment of the game, they are not essential.

C. FUNDAMENTALS OF TEACHING BASKETBALL

Teaching to be good should be interesting. Many potential basketball players drop by the wayside because of lack of interest. This lack of interest is usually brought about by poor teaching.

The teaching of techniques in basketball is of utmost importance if good basketball is to be played. The teaching and learning of these techniques may be very dull or very interesting. To be interesting they must be meaningful. To accomplish this the techniques should be taught and learned after their need has been shown and realized. A good basketball practice should start by a short playing period followed by practice of techniques and finished by another playing period. Techniques that need practice may be pointed out during the first playing period then practiced and put into actual play in the final playing period.

Very often teachers spend much time and energy teaching techniques as separate items unto themselves and never show their use in a game or see that they are incorporated in the actual play. Unless this is done little or no benefit comes from the fundamentals practiced. Techniques should be taught in as near gamelike situations as possible. Practices should be chosen in which players are made to move to meet the ball. The use of stationary practices for passes, shooting, pivoting, etc. is detrimental to players and promotes a static type of game. It is of extreme importance that this type of teaching be used with beginning, as well as advanced players. Once the habit of standing still to receive the ball is established, it is extremely difficult to prevent a player from feeling it necessary to be standing motionless when receiving the ball and when shooting.

Basketball can be, and is by some teams, played with little or no employment of fundamentals, techniques and tactics. This kind of basketball is usually very uninteresting and dull. Players should be inspired to learn and use good techniques and tactics through a desire to play a better game. A person always enjoys most those things which he can do best.

Adequate use of equipment should be made during practice sessions. If enough balls are available not more than six players (in

most practices) should be used in a squad. If a large number of
players must be handled at one time, and only one floor is available,
players may be divided into two teams and a game of "keep away"
played (using basketball rules) at the beginning of the practice to
get players warmed up. Then set up technique practice around the
edges of the playing court and let players rotate, keeping two teams
playing the entire time. Many players may be handled in this way
and all can have a chance to play as well as practice fundamentals.
In order to teach rules and interest players in officiating, it is well
to let players both officiate and observe others play and officiate.
This may easily be worked in as one of the squad rotations along
with playing and practicing.

CHAPTER II

CATCHING AND PASSING

CORRECT CATCHING IS ESSENTIAL to good passing. Since it is not possible to practice passing without catching, the instructor should stress correct catching in all practices. The proper mechanics of the body should be taught so that the player handles her body with grace and ease. The player who moves with grace and ease is the one who is efficient and conserves energy.

Points to Be Remembered:

1. Keep your eyes on the ball until it is caught.

2. Give with the ball. Keep fingers spread, wrists and elbows slightly flexed, and body poised but relaxed.

3. In catching, "give" to that position from which the ball will be thrown. Make catching and passing a continuous movement.

4. Spread the fingers; turning the palms toward the ball. In receiving a pass above the waist, the fingers should be pointed up. In receiving passes below the waist, the fingers should be pointed down.

5. Passes will be more accurate, and easier to handle by the receiver, if the cushions of the fingers control the ball rather than the palms of the hands. While it is true that girls need the palms of the hands for catching, the control in passing comes from the fingers. Therefore it is important that one learn to shift the ball easily, after it has been caught, so that the fingers can control the ball in passing.

6. Keep the elbows slightly bent, and as the ball contacts the fingers, bring them in fairly close to sides of the body. Many girls, when catching balls at about chest height, bend the wrists too much and force the elbows out to the side. This should be avoided, and can be, if the body gives with the impact of the ball.

7. When jumping to catch balls over the head, reach and catch with one hand whenever possible. The other hand is brought onto the ball as it is drawn down.

8. Whenever possible get into position so that hands and body are behind the ball.

6

9. Always go to meet a pass. Do not wait for the ball to come to you.

PASSING

In the descriptions given in this section, the individual making the pass is standing still. As soon as the mechanics of the pass have been learned, passing practice should, as far as possible, approximate game situations. Stationary passing practice should be completely eliminated after mechanics have been learned. Ability to pass with either hand is a decided asset and no player can consider herself well equipped unless she can pass with either hand.

Points to Be Remembered:

1. Always throw a pass ahead of the runner. *Make* her run to receive the ball. Don't cause her to slacken her speed or wait for it.

2. If passing with the right hand, it is usually easier to execute a pass if the left foot is forward, but players should learn to pass with either foot forward.

3. Master and use a variety of passes. Don't put all your power behind a pass going to a player near you. Control your speed and give her a pass which she can handle. The receiver will probably fumble a ball which comes hard and fast. The passer should help the receiver by making the ball float into the receiver's hands. This is done by controlling the ball with the cushions of the fingers, rather than with the palms of the hands.

4. The short pass is usually safer and more easily handled by the receiver.

Two-Hand Underhand Pass

Description:

1. This pass may be made with the ball on the side or in front of the body.

2. Feet are in forward backward, or side stride position.

3. Ball is held close to the body, at height of hips or lower, between both hands, palms facing, and fingers pointed down.

4. The arms are swung forward, upward, and the ball is released with a snap of the wrists as the weight is transferred to the forward foot.

5. This pass may be sent forward, in which case the wrists are snapped so that the fingers point forward, or it may be a pass backward, in which case the wrists are snapped so that the fingers point to the floor and backward.

Two-Hand Underhand Pass

Uses:

1. It is easy to control and therefore useful when passing to a player who is running close to you.

2. Since it is easy to guard it should not be used when passing across the floor, especially in your opponent's scoring zone.

3. This pass when directed backward is very useful if a player is caught at center line with back to her own goal.

Two-Hand Underhand Pass

One-Hand Underhand Pass ✗

Description:

1. Feet are in a forward backward, or side stride position.

2. Hand is low at side and slightly back of body. Elbow is almost straight (fingers are pointed down), with ball cupped in hand, facing the direction of the throw.

3. The arm is swung forward as the ball is released either with or without a snap of the wrist. The weight transfers to the forward foot.

One-Hand Underhand Pass

Uses:

1. To give a short pass to a player who is coming toward you, if you are closely guarded from the front or side.

2. Often used following a feint.

One-Hand Shoulder Push Pass

Description:

1. Ball is held in one hand, right elbow bent and low, back of hand in front of right shoulder, feet in forward backward stride position. (Ball may also be held to side of shoulder, or just behind and above shoulder.)

2. As the ball is pushed forward the weight of the body transfers to the forward foot. The elbow, wrist and fingers extend as the pass is made. The speed of the pass is determined by the amount of snap given by the fingers and wrist as the ball leaves the hands.

One-Hand Shoulder Push Pass

3. This pass may be directed forward or looped high; in the latter case there is no wrist snap, all the control coming from the fingers.

One-Hand Shoulder Push Pass

Uses:

1. Probably used more than any other pass. It is easy to control and is good as a quick pass to a player who is cutting for the basket.

2. Since it is easy to control and direct it is a good pass to any player who is receiving on the run anywhere on the floor.

One-Hand Chest Pass

Description:

Same as the one hand shoulder push pass except that the ball is held directly in front of the chest and is pushed forward or upward from that position.

Uses:

While the uses of this pass are limited it is effective in order:

1. To loop the ball over the head of a player, unless that player is guarding over the ball.

2. This is good for short passes especially if your opponent is coming in from the side and you can get rid of the ball before she crosses in front of you.

Two-Hand Chest Pass

Description:

1. Feet are in a forward backward stride position with most of body weight on forward foot.

2. The ball is held in both hands, fingers well spread, with the heel of the hand off the ball. The fingers grip the ball and the wrists are very slightly bent.

3. This pass may start with the ball in front of the chest or with the ball low, elbows slightly bent. In the latter case the elbows bend, remaining close to the sides of body and the ball is lifted to the chest before it is released.

4. The receiver can handle this pass most effectively if it reaches her between waist and shoulders. Therefore whether the pass is to be a straight line pass or an arched pass it should be directed to reach the upper half of her body.

5. The ball is released by extending the arms forward for a straight line pass, and upward for an arched pass.

6. In making the complete catch and chest pass the elbows describe a small circle starting backwards. The elbows are always kept fairly close to the sides of the body.

Two-Hand Chest Pass

Uses:

1. This pass is used very freely by teams using short, quick passes. It is especially valuable in the scoring area where it often follows a bounce.

2. This is a good pass to use by a player who has pivoted, when the person to whom she is passing is cutting across in front of her.

Two-Hand Overhead Pass

Description:

1. The ball is held overhead in two hands with palms facing, or with the hands behind the ball, fingers spread. The elbows are slightly bent.

2. The ball is released by snapping it forward using the wrists and the fingers.

3. The practice of carrying the ball backward, low behind the head, before it is snapped forward, should be discouraged.

Uses:

1. If the ball is caught high above the head, it is of value for shooting or passing because it can be released very quickly, and from the height of the jump.

Two-Hand Overhead Pass

2. Beginners in basketball often resort to this pass when guarded. In these cases the ball is dropped behind the head, causing the player to bend backward. This causes an unnecessary strain on the player and makes for a very slow game. Therefore its use should be discouraged until the player has acquired sufficient skill to make the pass, using the snap of the wrists, without bringing the ball low in back.

3. When closely guarded, this pass is a very valuable one if properly done.

One-Hand Overhead Pass

Description:

1. The ball is held in one hand, over the head, with the elbow and wrist bent. The palm is facing forward, with the fingers gripping and spread behind the ball.

2. The ball is released by swinging the arm forward and slightly downward, in the direction in which the pass is to be made, with a definite snap of the wrist as the ball leaves the hand.

One-Hand Overhead Pass

Uses:

1. This is a fast pass to a player who is cutting for the basket.

2. Defensive players find it useful in getting the ball away from opponents' scoring zone and into own forward section.

3. Because this can be a long fast pass it is valuable for a quick break from defense to offense.

4. If the space out of bounds is limited the pass is effective in playing the ball from out of bounds.

Two Hand Pass—Across Chest

Description:

1. In passing from the right side the ball is held in both hands, palms facing, with the right hand under the ball and the left hand on top. The fingers are spread, and the elbows bent. (The body twists to the right, from the waist as the ball is brought back to the right side.) The right elbow is forward.

2. The ball is released with a forceful extension of the elbows and a snap of the wrists, with the fingers giving it control and added impetus.

Two-Hand Pass—Across Chest

Uses:

1. When guarded on one side this pass may be used for a fast pass to a player who is running across in front. The pass is easy to direct from either right or left shoulder.

2. If a bounce has been taken on the right, and the opponent is following closely, this pass may be used by a player coming up court, toward the pass on the left.

3. This pass may also be developed into a bounce pass. When it is used as a bounce pass, the pass starts with the ball brought down to the shoulder. The ability to use this pass gives added versatility to a player.

Hook Pass

Description:

1. In this pass the foot work is most important. This is a difficult pass to execute and direct accurately when the body is well balanced. It is almost impossible to execute it if the body is off balance.

2. When the pass is taken the player's left side is in the direction to which the throw is to be made. The ball is held in two hands, waist height, fingers spread. The ball rests in the right hand, left hand helping to balance it, and the player is looking over her left shoulder.

3. Using a short step, the left foot is brought across the body, further to the left, knees well bent, with the body in a half crouch. The ball has been brought further around toward the right thigh.

4. As the player starts to make the throw the left hand comes off the ball, and the ball rests on the wrist of the right hand. As the player pivots high on the left foot preparatory to a high jump in the air, the ball is brought past the right shoulder, over the head and is passed from right to left over the left shoulder.

Hook Pass

5. The ball is released with a forceful snap of the wrist, as the left shoulder is lowered.

6. The player has jumped into the air, off her left foot, the body has been thrown in the direction of the pass, with the right arm, shoulder and leg being carried forward.

7. The player lands first on her right foot, and then on her left ready to follow the play.

Hook Pass

Uses:

1. This is a difficult pass for the opponent to block, particularly because as the passer crosses her left foot over, she draws her opponent out of her guarding position.

2. This is a good pass to a player who is cutting for basket, especially if the defense player guards closely, or is very tall.

Forward Bounce Pass

Description:

1. The bounce pass may be made with one or two hands. If made with one, the ball is held in two hands, and just before it is released, one hand leaves the ball as the other hand pushes it toward the floor.

2. The hand is on top and slightly behind the ball with the fingers spread. The elbow is bent to start, and straightens as the foot steps forward. The body is inclined forward following behind the ball.

3. The ball should strike the floor about one yard in front of the receiver.

4. Unless this pass is sharp and accurate, it makes for slow passing.

Forward Bounce Pass

Forward Bounce

Uses:

1. This pass lends variety to short passes to work the ball down the field.

2. It is especially valuable if used in passing to a player who is cutting for the basket because it is easy for the receiver to handle.

3. It is a good pass to use when passing the ball in from out of bounds under own basket.

4. This gives variety and avoids interception by a defensive player who is standing between you and a receiving teammate.

Forward Bounce

Backward Bounce Pass

Description:

1. This pass is used less by girls than by boys. It is a little harder to do than the forward bounce pass.

2. The ball is held in two hands, fingers spread. The left foot is diagonally forward to the left with most of the body weight on it. The ball is brought to the right side and as the left hand leaves the ball, the right hand is brought on top and slightly in front of the ball.

3. The ball is released by pushing it backward.

Uses:

1. While moving forward, the opponents are deceived by this backward bounce pass.

2. It is easy to evade an opponent by passing back and then circling around opponent to get into position to receive again.

Two-Hand Bounce Pass—Across Chest

(See two-hand pass across chest, p. 16)

Key for Diagrams

① ② ③	**OFFENSIVE PLAYERS**
☐1 ☐2 ☐3	**DEFENSIVE PLAYERS**
③→③	**PATH OF PLAYER**
--→	**PATH OF BALL**
⌢	**BOUNCE**
⌒ ⌒	**PIVOTS**
⌇⌇	**JUGGLE**

Practice 1

Gives Practice In:

   a. Passing ahead to a moving player.

   b. Catching while running.

   c. Following behind receiver.

   d. Moving as soon as ball leaves hand, and stopping as soon as ball is received.

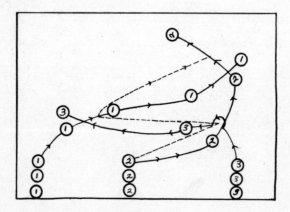

Description:

   Number 2 has ball. Numbers 1 and 3 run ahead.

   Number 2 passes to 3 and runs behind her.

   Numbers 1 and 2 run ahead.

   Number 3 passes to 1 and runs behind 1.

   Process continues indefinitely.

Practice 2

Gives Practice In:

  a. Passing ahead of receiver with accuracy.

  b. Avoiding running with the ball.

  c. Catching while running.

  d. Passing with speed.

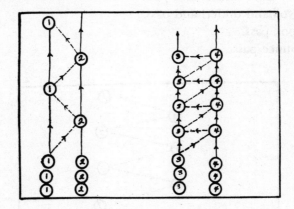

Description:

  Group divided into teams of 6 players each.

  Definite area marked off.

  First two players on each team run forward, passing while advancing.

  Object—Each team tries to make the greatest number of completed passes while running at full speed.

Practice 3

Gives Practice In:

Accurate passing, using:

    a. Chest pass.
    b. Push pass.
    c. One-hand overhead pass.
    d. One-hand underhand pass.
    e. Two-hand underhand pass.
    f. Hook pass.
    g. Bounce pass.

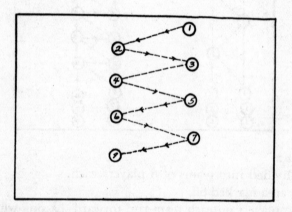

Description:

Players in two columns.

Starting with Number 1, pass diagonally down to end and back. Each time ball completes circuit, change the type of pass.

Practice 4

Gives Practice In:

Same as Practice 3 with the addition of:

    a. Passing while running.

    b. Receiving while running.

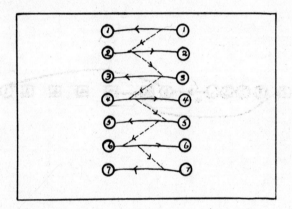

Description:

Formation same as Practice 3.

After Number 1 has made the pass to Number 2, who has run out to receive it, Number 1 runs over to opposite side. Number 2 passes to 3 and runs to opposite side.

Practice 5

Gives Practice In:

  a. Catching ball on run.

  b. Accuracy in passing to a receiver who is running toward passer.

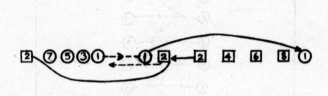

Description:

  Players in two columns.

  Number one passes to 2 who has run to receive pass.

  Number 2 passes to 3 who has run to receive pass.

  Same procedure used for as many players as are in columns.

CHAPTER III

INDIVIDUAL TECHNIQUES OR TACTICS

THE BOUNCE

Starting with the ball in two hands, one, usually the right, is on top and slightly behind the ball, the other under it. The player gives impetus to the ball causing it to bound on the floor, and recovers it before another player touches it.

Points to be Remembered:
1. The body should be behind the ball.
2. The fingers should be well spread as the ball is pushed, not slapped. The bounce is started from waist height, since holding it higher makes interception easier, and the arm extends forward as the ball is pushed toward the floor.
3. The angle at which the ball is sent to the floor determines the distance of the bounce. Players should try to gain distance on the bounce.
4. The force with which the ball is pushed determines the speed of the bounce.
5. The head should be kept up. The player must watch the other players on the court so that she may anticipate and avoid possible interception by an opponent.
6. A pass is faster than a bounce.
7. Many times good chances to shoot or pass are lost because the bounce is used when the situation does not warrant it.

Uses:
1. To gain distance.
2. To get nearer the basket to shoot.
3. To avoid an opponent, thus freeing oneself for passing or shooting.
4. To allow time for a team mate to get free of her opponent, so that she may receive a pass.
5. Combined with a feint or pivot, or both, it is an excellent way of "losing" an opponent.

Interception of the Bounce

6. *Note:* Too often players bounce from sheer habit; a bounce should be used only when needed. Beginners are prone to overuse this technique. When this happens it is suggested that players be forced to play without bouncing during practice.

Defense Against the Bounce:

1. A player should always attempt to intercept a bounce. This may result in either gaining possession of the ball, or a tie ball; either is certainly worth a try.

2. The most efficient way to intercept is with *one* hand (that hand nearest opponent) pulling the ball out to the side. The shoulder on side nearest opponent should be kept low and body turned slightly toward opponent. Hand on side nearest opponent is low on the ball to avoid fouling.

3. In intercepting a bounce it is easier to avoid fouling if the defensive player is not playing too close to her opponent.

4. Reach out to intercept with the hand nearest the opponent, but be sure to have the other hand across your own body, ready to place it on the ball as soon as the interception succeeds.

THE PIVOT

Pivoting is turning in any desired direction while keeping one foot at its initial point of contact with the floor. For sake of clarification the pivot is classified as follows:

a. Rear Pivot—turning either to right or left with the back leading; usually used when guarded from in front.

b. Front Pivot—Turning forward either to right or left; usually used when being guarded from the rear.

Points to be Remembered:

1. Knees should be slightly bent.

2. Pivot should be made away from, and not into, opponent.

3. Player should look and sense position of other players before executing a pivot.

4. An ability to pivot is essential and useful to every member of a team.

5. Players should be able to execute either front or rear pivot on either foot with equal ease.

6. Weight should be kept on pivot foot, and the pivot should be made on the *ball* of the foot.

Uses:

1. Frees a player so that she may bounce, pass, or shoot for basket.

2. It may be used either preceded or followed by a bounce as a means of evading an opponent.

3. It may be used either preceded or followed by a feint as a means of evading opponent.

4. This is an excellent technique for use by the defense to clear from under the basket.

5. A quick stop and pivot after a catch or bounce often throws off a trailing opponent.

6. A pivot is often useful when a player wishes to change direction.

Defense Against the Pivot:

1. Play far enough away from your opponent so that her body does not prevent or obstruct your chance to follow her.

2. Have your weight equally distributed and forward on toes, with knees slightly bent. The body is then ready to move in any direction and you will be able to stay with your opponent.

3. Anticipate your opponent's move.

4. Do not shift entire body weight to either foot too quickly. Your opponent may be feinting to throw your body weight to one side so she can reverse her play before you have recovered. Anticipate her play and shift your weight through the knees, not the feet. This makes it easier to recover and stop opponent from making pivot as she had planned.

THE JUGGLE

The ball is tossed into the air and is recovered by the player who originally gave impetus to the ball before it touches the floor or is touched by another player. It is usually executed over the head of an opponent.

Points to be Remembered:

1. When executing a juggle, player should transfer the ball to one hand before the toss, getting off to one side of her opponent.

Pivot

Pivot

This makes evasion of opponent easier and enables the player to get into position for a quick recovery of the ball.

2. The player using the juggle should look at the relative positions of other players on the court. Its use should be avoided when other players are likely to interfere.

3. The height of the juggle should be such as to prevent opponent from jumping or reaching up to intercept the ball, yet not so high that opponent has sufficient time to turn and intercept the ball as it descends.

4. The person making the juggle should recover the ball on op-

posite side of opponent as quickly as possible. A leap into the air often assures this recovery of the ball.

5. Juggles are easily intercepted. Practice is very necessary for their effective use.

6. Juggles are most effective if they follow a feint, that is, a feigned shot, pivot or pass.

Defense Against the Juggle:
1. Keep eyes on the ball.
2. Leap into the air and attempt to intercept as the ball is tossed, if the toss is low. If toss is high, pivot and attempt to intercept or at least tie the ball as it descends.

THE FEINT

The feint is a pretense to shoot, pass, pivot, or juggle in one direction with a quick change to the other direction or a change to another tactic.

Points to be Remembered:
1. After a feint change to other side quickly; otherwise, opponent has chance to regain balance and follow.
2. If after one feint, opponent follows too closely, feint to other side, or employ another tactic.
3. If opponent is not drawn on feint it is often best to continue with play to that side on which the feint was attempted.

Uses:
1. To pull an opponent off to one side before a pivot, bounce, pass, or shot, thus getting her off balance for guarding a play to the opposite side.
2. To get into position to receive a pass.

Defense Against the Feint:
1. Do not shift body weight to either foot too quickly.
2. Anticipate play and shift weight through the knees, not the feet. This makes it easier to recover and stop opponent from going in the direction she had planned.
3. Watch the shift of the body and not the ball.

Practice 6

Gives Practice In:

   a. Receiving on the run.

   b. Bouncing and passing to a moving receiver.

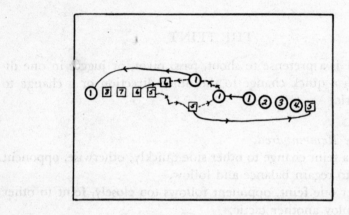

Description:

   Number 5 bounces ball and passes to Number 1 who has run out to meet it.

   Number 1 bounces ball and passes to number 6 who has run out to receive it.

   Number 1 goes behind 8 and 5 goes behind 4.

   Play continues indefinitely.

Practice 7

Gives Practice In:
   a. Bouncing.
   b. Pivoting.
   c. Accuracy in passing to a running receiver.

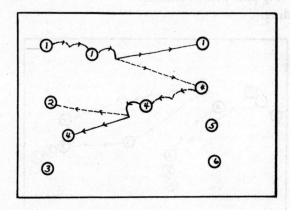

Description:

   Players in two columns.

   Number 1 bounces, pivots and passes to Number 4, then crosses over to 4's place.

   Number 4 bounces, pivots and passes to Number 2, then crosses over to 2's place.

   This continues down the line.

Practice 8

Gives Practice In:

a. Accuracy in passing while running.
b. Juggling.
c. Receiving pass while running.
d. Guarding.

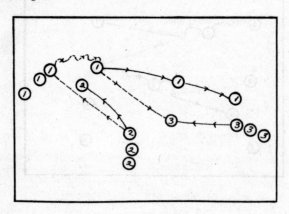

Description:

Number 2 has ball. Number 2 passes to Number 1 and runs in to guard her.

Number 1 juggles over 2 and passes to Number 3 who has run in to receive pass.

Number 1 then runs around behind 3 to 3's place.

Repeat same process with these positions, 2-3-1 instead of 1-2-3.

Practice 9

Gives Practice In:

   a. Bouncing.
   b. Guarding.
   c. Pivoting.
   d. Passing.

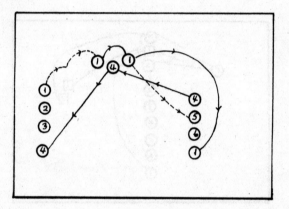

Description:

   Number 1 bounces out. Number 4 at the same time runs out to guard her.

   Number 1 pivots around 4 and passes back to Number 5.

   Number 5 now bounces out and 2 comes out to guard her.

   Number 1 goes behind 6 and 4 goes behind 3.

Practice 10

Gives Practice In:
 a. Catching while running.
 b. Guarding.
 c. Juggling.
 d. Intercepting juggle.

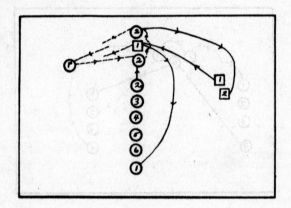

Description:
 Feeder throws ball to Number 2, who has run to receive it.
 Number 1 runs in to guard Number 2.
 Number 2 juggles over 1, while 1 tries to intercept.
 If juggle is completed, Number 2 passes to feeder; if not, Number 1 passes to feeder.

Practice 11

Gives Practice In:
- a. Passing to a running receiver.
- b. Running to meet a ball.
- c. Pivoting.
- d. Passing to side.

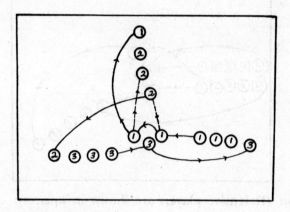

Description:

Number 2 passes to Number 1 who comes out to meet pass. Number 2 then goes to end of line 3.

Number 3 comes from opposite line to guard Number 1 who pivots past 3, and passes sideward to next Number 2. Number 1 goes to end of line 2, and 3 goes to end of line 1. Play continues until all are back in original places.

Practice 12

Gives Practice In:

 a. Passing and receiving on run.
 b. Hook pass.
 c. Bouncing, juggling or pivoting.
 d. Guarding.

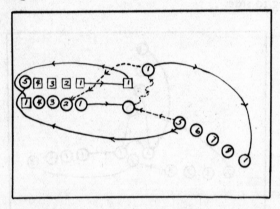

Description (Defensive players are shown in squares):

Offensive player Number 1 and defensive player Number 1 come out together.

Number 5 throws to 1 who juggles, bounces, or pivots past defensive 1 and throws a hook pass to offensive player Number 2 who comes out with defensive player Number 2 to receive it.

If defensive player 1 intercepts juggle or bounce of 1 she makes pass to 2.

Play continues until all have had several chances.

Practice 13

Gives Practice In:

a. Bouncing.

b. Catching ball on the run.

c. Accuracy in passing to a receiver who is running toward the passer.

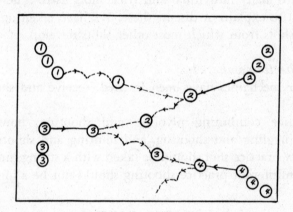

Description:

Players in two columns.

Number 1 bounces ball then passes to 2 who has run to receive the pass.

Number 2 bounces, then passes to 3 who has run to receive the pass.

Same procedure used for as many players as are in the four columns.

CHAPTER IV

SHOOTING

THERE ARE MANY ways of shooting and many different kinds of shots. The one desired end is to get the ball through the basket in a legal manner. Shots may be taken while the shooter is either stationary or in motion. Stationary shooting is good only when the shooter is not being guarded. If a player is apt in shooting while in motion, her opportunities for shooting will be increased. There is less chance of being guarded effectively if a player shoots while in motion.

There are many individual and trick shots used. There has been no attempt to explain or discuss these. We have taken only the fundamental shots from which most other shots develop.

Points to be Remembered:

1. After mechanics have been learned, receive and shoot on the run.

2. Practice combining pivoting and shooting, bouncing and shooting, juggling and shooting, and feinting and shooting.

3. Every practice shot should be taken with a strong intent to cage the ball. Indifferent practice shooting should not be allowed.

CHEST SHOT

This is usually a field shot taken some distance from the basket and may be taken either in motion or stationary depending on the situation. The chest shot is made in the same manner as the chest pass. Players using this shot should attempt to keep knees fairly straight. Too much knee bend is apt to spoil the shooter's aim. Note description of chest pass on page 13.

Points to be Remembered:

a. Eyes should be kept on the basket.

b. When shooting from in front and extreme side, ball should be arched so as to drop from above downward into the basket.

c. Shots taken from 45 degree angles (these are the most desirable angles) at the basket should be banked on back board slightly above and to the right or left of basket depending on side from which shot is taken.

d. Follow up shots should be taken when at all possible, particular effort should be made to follow field shots.[*]

Two-Hand Chest Shot

e. Chest shots should not be attempted when closely guarded from in front. To do so may cause the foul "charging" if the ball is pushed through opponent's hands.

TWO-HAND OVERHEAD SHOT

The same technique is used as in two-hand overhead pass. Note description of pass on page 14.

This shot is used after a player has received a very high pass near the basket. When executed properly the player releases ball with snap of wrist, and at the height of the jump.

If done by leaning way back and dropping arms and ball behind head this shot is very easily guarded, hard to control, inaccurate, usually very slow, and the shooter is off-balance for follow-up shot.

Two-Hand
Overhead Shot

Two-Hand Overhead Shot

This shot is often resorted to by beginners due to lack of training in other shots. Its use should be discouraged for beginners.

ONE-HAND HOOK SHOT

The same technique is used as in one-hand hook pass. Note description on page 17.

It is often used when side is toward basket and opponent is between shooter and basket.

It is executed with one hand and over the head.

It is a very difficult shot to guard and is also a very difficult shot to make.

One-Hand Hook Shot

Progression of Hook Shot Starting with Back to Basket, Turn and Follow Through

ONE-HAND PUSH SHOTS UNDER THE BASKET

Taken very close to the basket and usually while in motion; for player is generally cutting in toward basket. For the sake of clarification these shots are classified as follows:

a. One-Hand Push Shot running in from right.

b. One-Hand Push Shot running in from left.

c. One-Hand Push Shot running in from in front.

d. One-Hand Push Shot running in from left to right across basket.

e. One-Hand Push Shot running in from right to left across basket.

Points to be Remembered:

a. Keep eyes on the basket.

b. Release ball at height of jump. The closer the player is to the basket when shot is made, the easier the shot.

c. The ball should be banked on back board a little above and to the right or left depending on side from which the shot is taken. Exception to this rule is the shot from in front, in which case the ball should be looped just over the rim of the basket.

d. The ball should be transferred to one hand. Shooting with one hand allows for greater height and reach on jump.

e. Arm holding the ball should reach toward basket as jump is made.

f. The efficient under basket shooter is the one who shoots equally well with either right or left hand. Note picture.

One-Hand Push Running in
Front Right

Shifting of Ball in Preparation for One-Hand Shots

Progression One-Hand Push Shot Running in from Right

One-Hand Push Shot Running
in Front Left

One-Hand Push Shot Running in
from Left Using Left Hand

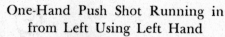

One-Hand Push Shot Running in
from Front

One-Hand Push Shot Running in
from Left to Right Across Basket

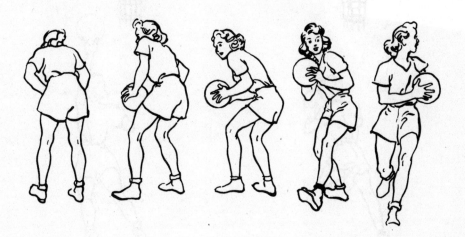

Pivot Turn, Shoot, One-Hand Push Shot

One-Hand Push Shot Running from Left to Right Across Basket

One-Hand Push Shot Running from Right to Left Across Basket

TWO-HAND UNDERHAND SHOT

Same technique is used as in Two-Hand Underhand pass. Note the description on page 7. This shot should be used only when unguarded.

FOUL SHOTS

Of the possible ways to shoot fouls there is no type which should be prescribed for all players.

A player should try them all out and choose that one which seems the easiest and most efficient for her. This shot should be practiced until the player masters it.

Possible shots used for foul shooting:

a. Chest.

b. Two-Hand Underhand.

Foul shooting should not be neglected in practice. The aim should be to convert every foul shot into a point. To do this one must practice regularly.

When practicing foul shots a player should not stand in the same spot without moving during the entire practice. After each shot she

Chest Shots

Forward Backward Stride   Side Stride

Two-Hand Underhand Shots
Forward Backward Stride　　　　　　　　　Side Stride

should step away from foul line. In a game one must walk up to the line anew for each shot (with exception of double shot award). Where possible make all practice simulate game conditions.

A good method of keeping the players interested in shooting fouls for practice is to keep a chart or card file in which each girl records the number of foul shots taken and the number made at every practice. In this way the player may watch her own progress or lack of progress.

Practice 14

Gives Practice In:
  a. Bouncing.
  b. One hand under basket shots.
  c. Recovering ball from backboard.
  d. Pivoting away from backboard.

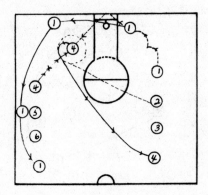

Description:

Number 1 bounces and shoots, using right hand one hand shot.

Number 4 recovers ball from backboard, pivots and passes to Number 2.

Number 1 goes behind Number 6, and Number 4 goes behind 3.

Number 2 bounces and shoots and Number 5 recovers, etc.

Practice 15

Gives Practice In:
  a. Bouncing.
  b. Cross basket shots.
  c. Recovering ball from backboard.
  d. Accuracy in passing.

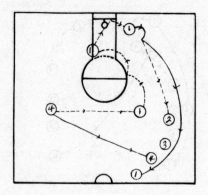

Description:
  Number 4 passes to Number 1.
  Number 1 bounces into position for a cross basket shot, shoots and recovers ball and passes to Number 2.
  Number 4 takes place behind Number 3 and Number 1 lines up behind 4.

Practice 16

Gives Practice In:
  a. Accuracy in making two hand under hand side pass or flip.
  b. Receiving short passes.
  c. Bouncing.
  d. Cross-basket shots.

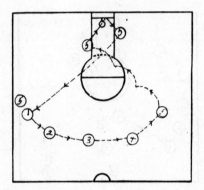

Description:

Using a two hand underhand side pass or flip Number 1 passes to Number 2, 2 passes to 3, etc., until ball reaches number 5.

Number 5 bounces cross-basket and takes a cross-basket shot from left.

Number 5 takes Number 1's place, line rotates so that Number 4 is in Number 5's place.

Practice 17

Gives Practice In:
   a. Bouncing.
   b. Shooting.
   c. Recovering ball from backboard.
   d. Guarding.

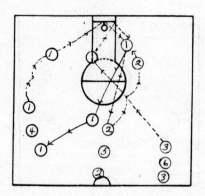

Description:

Number 1 bounces, shoots, recovers, and passes to Number 2.

Number 1 then runs back to guard Number 2.

Number 2 bounces past 1, shoots, recovers, and passes to Number 3, and runs to guard her. Number 3 does the same and passes to Number 4, etc.

Practice 18

Gives Practice In:
  a. Stopping quickly after run.
  b. Pivoting to evade opponent.
  c. Cutting toward opponent.
  d. Receiving pass while running.
  e. Bouncing.
  f. Following up another player's shot.

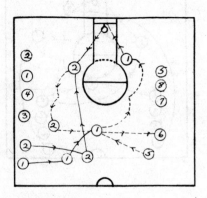

Description:

Number 1 and 2 run out together.

Number 1 stops quickly, pivots, and cuts toward basket to receive pass from Number 5. After receiving pass she bounces and shoots. Number 2 follows up shot, bounces out, and passes to 5, who comes out with 6. Play is repeated until all players are back in original places.

Practice 19

Gives Practice In:
   a. Bounce pass.
   b. Catching while running.
   c. Bouncing.
   d. Shooting.
   e. Guarding.
   f. Passing.
   g. Juggling.

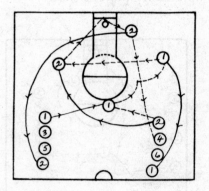

Description:

Number 2 has ball and passes to Number 1 who has run out to meet the pass. Number 1 bounces and passes with a bounce pass to 2 who has run up to meet pass, and then Number 1 runs up to guard her.

Number 2 bounces past Number 1 toward basket and shoots, recovers and passes back to 4.

Number 2 goes behind 5 and Number 1 goes behind 6.

Practice same starting with a juggle and bounce pass.

Practice 20

Gives Practice In:
  a. Pivoting.
  b. Pick-off.
  c. Bouncing.
  d. Shooting.
  e. Receiving while running.

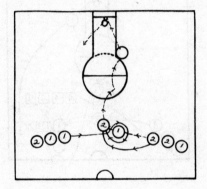

Description:

Number 2 passes to Number 1 who has run to receive pass.

Number 1 pivots while 2 runs behind her to take a pick-off pass from 1.

Number 2 bounces and shoots, and goes to end of line.

Number 1 recovers ball and passes back to Number 2 line.

Practice 21

Gives Practice In:

   a. Juggling, cutting for basket.

   b. Catching while running.

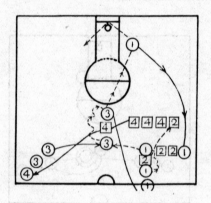

Description:

   Number 1 juggles over 2 who is guarding her, and passes to 3 who has run in to receive ball.

   Number 3 juggles over 4 who has run in to guard, and passes to 1 who has cut toward basket to receive ball.

Practice 22

Gives Practice In:

   a. Accuracy in passing while running.

   b. Recovering ball from backboard.

   c. Cutting for basket.

   d. Pivoting away from center of court after recovery from back board.

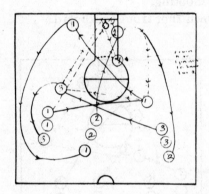

Description:

This play may start from either side, depending on which side the ball is recovered from the board. In this description the play starts from the left.

Number 1 shoots. 1, 2 and 3 then start to move simultaneously to execute the following: 2 runs forward and recovers ball from the backboard, pivots away from center of court, and passes to 1 who has run cross-court interchanging with 3.

Number 1 passes to 3 who started to cut for basket when 1 received the ball. As soon as 3 receives the ball she shoots, does not follow her shot but turns and circles around and back to line 1.

Number 1 recovers ball from backboard and passes to first person in line on side toward which she pivots. She then goes to line 2.

Practice 23

Gives Practice In:

    a. Receiving ball when guarded.
    b. Accuracy in passing.
    c. Guarding.
    d. Accuracy in shooting.
    e. Recovering own shot from backboard.

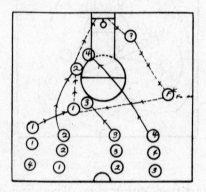

Description:

    Feeder throws ball into center.

    Numbers 1, 2, 3 and 4 run in.

    Number 1 receives ball and passes it to Number 2 who has cut toward basket.

    Number 2 shoots.

    Numbers 3 and 4 act as guards but if they intercept they shoot and recover, passing back to feeder.

Practice 24

Gives Practice In:
  a. **Cutting for basket, passing, receiving.**
  b. **Bouncing, pivoting.**

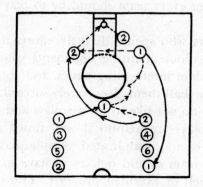

Description:

Number 1 cuts for basket and receives pass from Number 2. Number 1 bounces in, pivots, and passes across to 2, who has cut in under basket. Number 2 shoots, follows shot, passes back to 4. Number 1 goes behind 6, 2 behind 5.

CHAPTER V

OFFENSE

QUICK STOPPING, starting, ability to change direction, and efficient handling of the ball is essential for a good offensive or defensive player. The offensive player or forward must have (in addition to these skills) the ability to shoot and make baskets.

The team which is in possession of the ball is the offensive team. Since the best defense is a good offense, the essential thing is to keep possession of the ball and if it is lost to regain it as quickly as possible. A team may score only when in possession of the ball, therefore the aim of every team should be to play offensive basketball.

Teams or players who spend all their efforts in defensive play, running about the floor guarding opponents who have possession of the ball, but seldom intercepting passes, and obtaining and keeping possession of the ball themselves, rarely succeed.

Some instructors do not like to use set plays and team formations. We believe floor plays are helpful if well timed and worked out. These should not be too complicated. Simple plays are better and more workable. A team should not try to have so many plays that none are known well or executed properly. Two or three are usually enough; more tend to confuse the players. A few set plays properly executed are much better than many plays, none of which is usable in the excitement of a game.

Good timing is the most important factor in successful team plays. If a receiver gets to a spot before the ball, she will usually be covered by an opponent; if she gets there too late her teammate in possession of the ball will be covered, thus making passing difficult. Many teams are unable to use floor plays because of lack of practice and understanding of timing.

It is true that a team cannot play a whole game without some impulsive playing. A team which cannot rise to unforeseen situations and play without set plays would be at a great loss. Ideally a team should be able to fall into this type of play when the occasion demands and also be able to execute plays and gain the advantage from them when possible.

The individual who is skillful as an individual player is of no team value unless she can adapt her style of play to the team as a whole. Every member of the team should know the style of play of every other member. She should know their strengths as well as their weaknesses.

Points to be Remembered:

1. Good passing is the outstanding characteristic of a good offensive team.

2. The player making the pass is often responsible for the receiver's fumble. The receiver should keep her eye on ball until it is in her possession.

3. Short passes directed ahead of the receiving player will do much to keep a team on the move.

4. Rarely pass to a player who is standing still unless she is free for a set shot at goal. The chances of having the pass intercepted are too great.

5. Avoid corners and lines, since your field of action is limited if you are caught in these positions. Always leave yourself enough room to move in at least two directions.

6. Do not use a bounce if your opponent is guarding you loosely. It is too easy for her to take your bounce away from you entirely or to tie the ball.

7. If you are balanced and in position for a shot, and have a yard between yourself and your opponent, shoot.

8. Do not shoot unless you are in position. You cannot afford to lose the ball. Pass to a teammate.

9. If a guard raises her hand to stop your shot, quickly bounce ball past her on the side on which her arm is raised.

10. Work yourself and your opponent away from the shooting area if you are going to pass to a player who is cutting for basket. This not only gives her room but also eliminates the chances of having the extra guard in for a shift by the defense.

11. If you have shot and your teammate is in a good position to follow the shot, stay out because you bring another defensive player with you.

12. If you do follow up a shot and are not in a position to shoot, pass to a teammate and then come out. Avoid crowding under the basket.

13. Take all out-of-bounds balls quickly.

14. A juggle is a slow play and should not be overdone. It is a good deceptive play if used wisely.

15. Don't bounce if you can pass advantageously. Your opponent gains time and can cover you. A pass is faster.

16. On foul shots, if you are not shooting, don't get caught with your weight on your heels. Be ready to jump and get the ball from the backboard or tap it back to the foul shooter or the other forward.

17. In the first few minutes of each half you should have planned your attack on the basis of the things you have learned about your opponents' style of play. You should know their special strengths and weaknesses and be prepared to change your style of play to combat theirs.

18. Signals are helpful on plays from center and from out-of-bounds. But players must be ready to drop a planned play and substitute some other maneuver if the planned play does not work.

19. Let the person best qualified to give signals do so. Some prefer having forwards give signals, others prefer guards. This depends on the place and on the particular group of players.

20. Do not use set plays without some variety. For example, if your team receives the ball out-of-bounds three times in a quarter do not use the same play every time. You might use it twice, but by the third time the defense will probably have planned to stop it.

21. Players should not waste their energy by aimless wandering. Every move should be purposeful though not obvious. Though you may not actually be passing or receiving you should contribute to the play by making spaces or by drawing opponents away from their fields of usefulness.

22. If learning the pick-off,* do not use the play in a game until you are letter perfect in its execution. The timing of the forward who picks-off must be perfect.

---

* Screening is a legal maneuver by which a player of the team in possession of the ball takes such a position on the floor so as to prevent a defensive player from guarding the player who has the ball. Picking-off, or screening, is not to be confused with blocking, which is illegal. Blocking is actually impeding the progress of an opponent who has not the ball, while in picking-off the opponent is caused to change the path she ordinarily would have taken to guard the player she desires to guard. Of course, when personal contact results from an intended pick-off, a foul must be called, but it may be on either the offensive or defensive player, depending on which seemed more at fault. The burden of responsibility for avoiding personal contact is on the player attempting to pick-off. A simple direct-pass pick-off play is shown in Practice 14, Page 53.

23. If opponents use zone defense and forwards find it impossible to break through, long shots should be attempted. If these shots are successful the defense will undoubtedly come out and the offense can then break through for short shots.

Play 1

Elements stressed in this play:
   a. Passing to a receiver who is running to meet the ball.
   b. Bouncing and shooting.

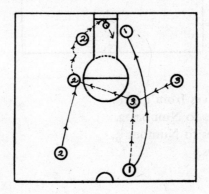

Description:
   Number 1 receives from the guard.

   Number 1 passes to Number 3.

   Number 3 passes to either Number 1 or Number 2 who run on either side of Number 3.

   Number 1 or Number 2 shoots after the bounce.

Play 2

Elements stressed in this play:

  a. Passing thru center of court.

  Shooting immediately after receiving pass.

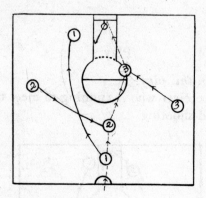

Description:

  Number 1 receives from guard.

  Number 1 passes to Number 2.

  Number 2 passes to Number 3.

  Number 3 shoots.

Play 3

Elements stressed in this play:
  a. Bouncing and shooting.
  b. Zig zag passing.

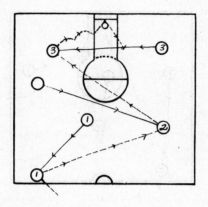

Description:

  Number 1 receives from guards and passes to Number 2:
  Number 2 passes to Number 3.
  Number 3 bounces and shoots.
  This play may be reversed to the other side.

Play 4

Elements stressed in this play:
    a. Passing to receiver who is running to meet the pass.
    b. Shooting.

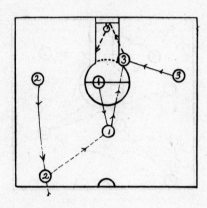

Description:
    Number 2 receives ball from the guard.
    Number 2 passes to Number 1.
    Number 1 passes to Number 3.
    Number 3 shoots.
    Entire play may be reversed to other side.

Play 5

Elements stressed in this play:
  a. Passing to receiver who is running to meet the pass.
  b. Pick-off.
  c. Shooting.

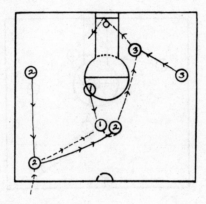

Description:
  Number 2 receives the ball from the guard.
  Number 2 passes to Number 1.
  Number 1 passes back to Number 2 on Pick-off.
  Number 2 passes to Number 3 who shoots.

Play 6

Elements stressed in this play:
   a. Passing to receiver who is running to meet pass.
   b. Pick-off.
   c. Shooting.

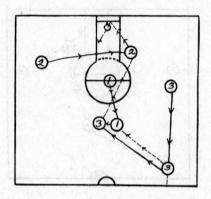

Description:
   Number 3 receives from the guard.
   Number 3 passes to Number 1.
   Number 1 passes back to Number 3 on Pick-off.
   Number 3 passes to Number 2 who shoots.

Play 7

Elements stressed in this floor play:
   a. Timing.
   b. Passing to player who is running to receive.
   c. Cutting toward basket on inside of court.

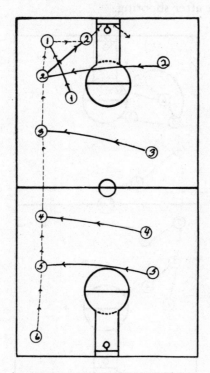

Description:

   Number 6 passes to Number 5. Number 5 passes to 4, 4 to 3, 3 to 2, 2 to 1.

   Number 1, using a loop or bounce pass, passes to Number 2 who cuts toward basket. Number 2 shoots.

Play 8

Elements stressed in this floor play:
  a. Timing.
  b. Passing to player who is running to receive.
  c. Running toward basket to follow other forward's shot.
  d. Staying out after shooting.

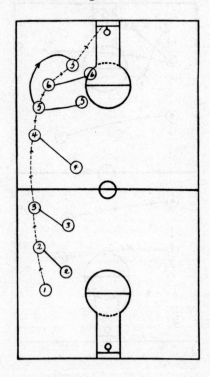

Description:
    Number 1 passes to 2. Number 2 passes to 3, 3 to 4, 4 to 5, 5 to 6.
    Number 5 runs around toward sideline and receives from 6.
    Number 6 runs toward basket to follow shot which 5 has tried.
    Number 5 stays out after she shoots.

Play 9

Elements stressed in this floor play:
   a.   Timing.
   b.   Zig zag passing.

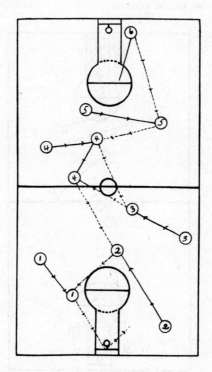

Description:
   Number 6 passes to 5, 5 to 4, 4 to 3, 3 back to 4, 4 to 2, 2 to 1.
   Number 1 shoots.

Play 10

Elements stressed in this floor play:
   a. Timing.
   b. Running to a definite space to receive pass.
   c. Receiving on pivot play.

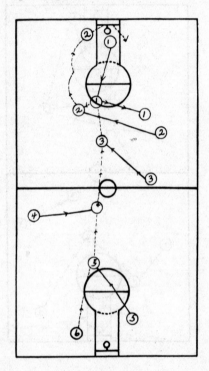

Description:
   Number 6 passes to 5, 5 to 4, 4 to 3, 3 to 1.

   Number 2 comes around Number 1 and receives a short pass from 1 as Number 1 pivots toward sideline. Number 2 bounces and shoots, or shoots without bouncing. Number 1 does not go in toward basket.

Play 11

Elements stressed in this floor play:
   a. Same as in play No. 10 in addition to
   b. Feint.

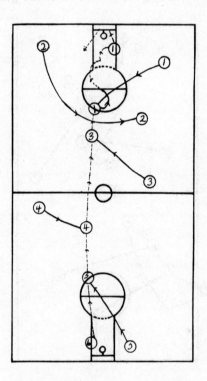

Description:

Same as play No. 10 until Number 1 receives it.

Number 1 feints and fakes a pass to Number 2 who has come around behind her.

Number 1 then pivots and bounces toward basket and shoots.

Play 12

Elements stressed in this floor play:

    a. Out of bounds play on side; in this play guard, 4, takes ball.

    b. Pivoting and changing direction, to evade guard.

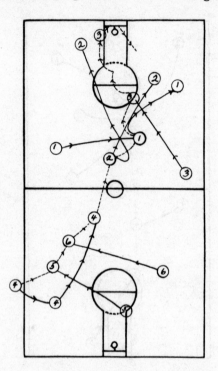

Description:

    Number 4 is out of bounds and passes to Number 5.

    Number 5 passes to 6, 6 to 4 and 4 to 2.

    Number 2 pivots right and passes to Number 1.

    Number 1 pivots left and passes to 3. Number 3 bounces and shoots.

Play 13

Elements stressed in this floor play:
  a. Accurately timed passes.
  b. Pivot play followed by bounce and pass.

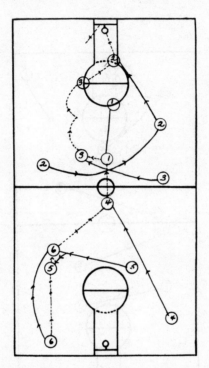

Description:

Number 6 passes to 5, 5 to 6, 6 to 4 and 4 to 1.

Number 1 pivots and gives a short pass to 3 who comes behind 1.

Number 3 bounces and passes to 2 who has cut across court from left to right and then toward basket from right to left.

Number 2 shoots from right under basket.

Play 14

Elements stressed in this floor play:
    a. Timing run.
    b. Accurate passing.
    c. Pivot.
    d. Pick-off.

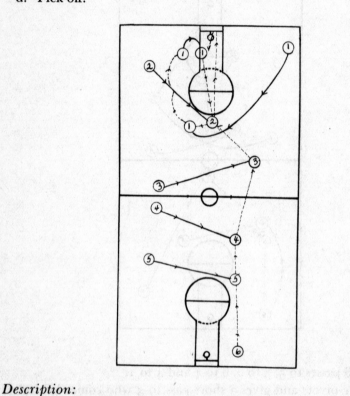

Description:

Number 6 passes to 5, 5 to 4, 4 to 3, 3 to 2.

Number 2 passes to 1 who has circled around behind her to receive a short pass as 2 pivots.

Number 1 bounces, pivots and passes to Number 2, who has faked a cut for basket, and has come back to the foul line. Number 2 shoots from here.

CHAPTER VI

DEFENSE

EITHER ZONE DEFENSE or man to man defense when used alone is impracticable. A combination of the two makes for the most effective defense. In man to man defense each player is assigned to one opponent and is responsible for that player and that player alone. In zone defense each player on the defensive team assumes responsibility for a certain area of the court and accepts any player coming into that area as her opponent. Should more than one opponent come into the same area at one time, the defensive player responsible for the area takes the first player who comes into the section. A free defensive player comes in to take the second offensive player.

There are various ways of dividing the court into guarding zones.

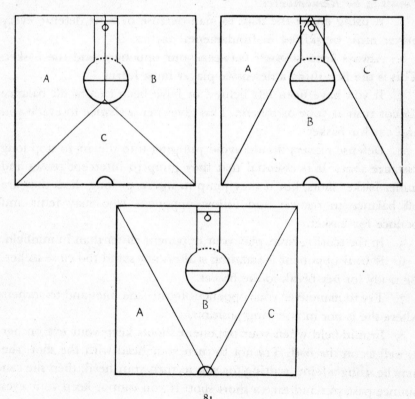

When to shift from the zone system to the man to man system of defense is a thing which must be worked out by each individual team. Defense is a matter of three players working together to prevent forwards from scoring. It is essential that the defensive players play together enough to thoroughly know each other's abilities and style of playing. Only after this sense of working together has been acquired can a good defense be worked out. It is the highest type of cooperative team play.

It is advisable to use the zone system as the offensive team receives the ball in its own half (forward zone) of the court. As the offensive players come near the basket man to man system is employed except that when screen plays are used by the offense the defensive players shift again as illustrated on page 81.

Points to be Remembered:

1. If using either the man to man defense or zone defense every player must be skilled in fundamental tactics.

2. Always keep yourself between your opponent and the basket. This is the first thing a defensive player must learn.

3. If you have been left behind or have been caught off balance do not rush at your opponent. This gives her a chance to evade you and cut for basket.

4. Defense players should avoid jumping into the air to stop long distance shots. It is essential that they jump to intercept passes and under basket shots, but if they jump to intercept long shots they are off balance to recover and follow opponent who may feint and bounce for basket.

5. In the scoring zone, play your opponent closer than in midfield.

6. If your opponent is standing still do not stand too close to her. Be ready for her break to the basket.

7. Try to maneuver your opponent to the side lines and to corners where she is not in a scoring position.

8. In mid-field when your opponent shoots keep your eye on her as well as on the ball. Try not to turn your head with the shot; she may be using a feint, waiting for you to turn your head, then she can bounce past you and take a short shot. If you cannot keep your eyes on both player and ball on a given play keep your eyes on the player. Avoid blocking.

9. When catching a ball protect it by pulling your body behind

it. This is especially important in taking balls off the backboard or when a bounce is used to carry the ball out from under the basket.

10. Don't let your player throw you off with a shift. She may pass the ball, start in one direction at full speed, then quickly stop, and step backward a few steps, to receive again. She is trying to get you going in the first direction, to receive and shoot or pass again before you have recovered.

11. To avoid fouling in intercepting a bounce the defense must keep the hand nearest opponent low or she will cause a foul by contact with her opponent's arm.

12. Watch for opponents' signals, but do not allow this to take your concentration from your defensive tactics. Often teams are so concerned over their opponents' signals that they miss opportunities to intercept passes.

13. Be ready for out-of-bounds plays. Don't let your opponents catch you napping.

14. In the first few minutes of each half, study your opponent's style of play. Find out if she always pivots on her right or left foot. Not all players are adept at pivoting on both feet.

15. If she bounces a great deal guard her loosely to intercept these bounces.

16. If she pivots a great deal guard her more closely to prevent her from pivoting.

17. Always keep your hand on the inside of the court low. Don't let her make you raise that arm so that she can feint past you on that side. Make her go to the outside of the court if she is going to pass you.

18. Keep your weight on your toes, do not shift with every move of your opponent. If she has the ball she has the advantage since she initiates the play and you must anticipate her movement.

19. If teams use the pick-off or pivot plays, guard your opponent closely so as to prevent the forward (not the one you are guarding) cutting between you and your opponent.

20. If a player succeeds in temporarily screening you from your opponent, switch to the other player and let your teammate switch to yours. Call out to your teammate for she may not see this play as quickly as you do.

21. Alert guards should never allow forwards to recover rebounds from backboard.

22. Defense should never pass ball across opponents' basket.

23. Defense players in clearing from under basket should always clear to sides of court.

24. A good defense will shift from defense to offense immediately upon possession of the ball.

25. When defensive players get possession of the ball and change to offense one of the guards should go or stay back near the basket while the other two carry the ball out toward their forwards. One player stays back as a "safety player" in the event that the other team intercepts a pass and attempts to cut for basket.

26. A team can score only when in possession of the ball. Consequently every effort should be made to obtain the ball before it gets to a player rather than guard the player after she has the ball.

Play 15

Elements stressed in this play:
   a. Switch of defense for pick-off play.

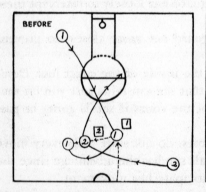 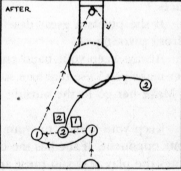

Description (Defensive players shown in squares):

As Number 1 starts to come around Number 2 to receive short pass, Number 1's guard moves over to take Number 2's forward and 2 is then able to cover 1's forward. If this principle of switching is learned by defensive players they will have little trouble in breaking up pivot and pick-off plays on the part of the offensive.

CHAPTER VII

OFFICIATING

IN 1932 A SURVEY made by the Women's Basketball Rules Committee revealed that while 92.76 per cent of the teams playing were using the women's rules, only 66 per cent employed women officials.

Many men who officiate at girls' games have studied the rules and have been intelligent and competent in interpreting them in games. However, it is the feeling of women who are interested in the girls who play basketball that they would rather have women officiating at women's games. How would men like to have women officials for men's games? Sounds amusing, doesn't it? Tradition says that women cannot officiate for men; but that men can officiate for women. This tradition evolved because in the early years of the game women were not trained as officials. Today major departments in physical education, and state teachers' colleges are offering courses not only in the technique of playing basketball but in the technique of officiating. There are approximately 65 local boards of women officials organized under the Women's National Officials Rating Committee to examine and rate officials in 33 states. No woman would presume to referee a man's game and now that the need for men officials for women's games no longer exists we wish the men felt the same way about refereeing for us.

In the Official Basketball Guide one will find full information about the Women's National Officials Rating Committee and an article for the woman official. The articles in this section of the Guide are written for the official who is actually officiating, but the ability to officiate must be learned or developed.

If one would learn to officiate for basketball games there is much one should do. Let us consider the qualifications of an official and then see if and how these qualities can be developed.

1. The official must have a thorough knowledge and understanding of the rules.

This can be acquired through study of the rules and playing the game. Both are essential. Interpretation meetings are held every year under the auspices of local boards of officials and anyone who would learn to officiate should attend these meetings to observe the effect that the latest rules changes will have on the playing.

2. Since maturity of judgment is essential it is necessary that the person learning to officiate be at least 16 years of age. Rarely does mature judgment come earlier.

3. She must inspire confidence and since her appearance and manner determine this to some extent she should have good posture and be neat in appearance and dress and efficient yet not aggressive in manner. Some officials have pleasing manners, others annoy the players because of their manner. No one can be a really good official unless she has a pleasant manner along with her efficiency in handling a game. This can be developed by critical self-evaluation and objective analysis of one's self.

4. She must have a good quick reaction time. This requires first, that she be in excellent physical condition, since no one can be alert unless one is in excellent health. While some people have through endowment quicker reaction time than others, and some can never learn to officiate well because they cannot acquire or develop it, others will find that concentration and practice will help considerably.

5. A good official must have a sense of humor and an appreciation of the players' point of view. This latter comes only through playing. The former can be developed if one does not take one's self too seriously. Officiating is a game and can be fun if you will look upon it as a game and not as a chore.

EQUIPMENT AND COSTUME

1. The Official Basketball Guide for the current year is an absolute necessity.

2. A loud, clear toned whistle. Most officials find that it is best to wear it on a ribbon or cord around the neck. How to blow your whistle is important. Hold it between your lips with the curved side down, tip of the tongue inserted in or against the slot. As the whistle is blown the tongue drops down out of the slot giving a short, sharp blast. With practice one learns to blow the whistle so that it is expressive. It talks for you.

3. Sport clothing which is distinct from either team is considered most appropriate. Sneakers or rubber soled shoes are essential.

4. If the game is being played out-of-doors it is wise to wear a visor to prevent the rays of the sun from striking the eyes.

THE GAME

After all preliminaries for the game have been arranged, and these are outlined in detail in the Basketball Guide for the current year, you are ready to start officiating.

1. Toss the ball to the center for the center throw. Blow your whistle when the center *receives* the ball, not when you throw it. The sounding of your whistle starts the game.

2. Keep moving with the play and concentrate on personal fouls. Call any violations you see but concentrate on personal fouls. Have some one on the side lines keep a record of fouls and violations called by you as well as a record of those you have missed. This can best be done by having that person put down a check every time you call a thing correctly, an x every time you miss a thing and a minus for everything you call incorrectly. Do not be discouraged when you find that you have been over-zealous. Experience will help you improve your score *if* you will concentrate and accept criticisms intelligently. Just as one cannot learn to play after only a few games, so one must practice officiating in many games before one becomes a competent official.

3. After one has learned to referee one should next learn to umpire. While the umpire often seems to have less to do than the referee, her job requires even more skill and judgment than the referee's. It is easier to follow the ball than to watch that part of the field to which the ball may be going or that part of the field from which the ball has come. Umpiring requires rare concentration. One cannot become interested in the progress of the ball. It is the most natural thing in the world to follow the play, and the ball, but the umpire's primary responsibility is to watch the fore-field and the backfield. In addition to doing this she must be ready to rule on out-of-bounds balls on her side of the court, and to toss for tie-balls which occur on her half of the court. Because umpiring is much more difficult to learn than refereeing we strongly recommend that when possible one concentrate on refereeing before attempting to umpire.

Date Due